THE BUSINESS STRATEGY GAME GUIDE

Learn the Essentials of BSG and How to Make Effective Decisions to Earn Your Degree

Derek J. Barnick

Copyright © 2020 Derek J. Barnick

All rights reserved.

No part of this book may be reproduced, or stored in a retrieval system, or transmitted in any form or by any means, electronic, mechanical, photocopying, recording, or otherwise, without express written permission of the publisher.

To request permissions, contact the publisher at djbarnick@gmail.com.

CONTENTS

Title Page	
Copyright	
Introduction	
Scoring	1
Choosing the Right Strategy	5
Compensation & Training	7
Branded Production	9
Production Facilities	12
Distribution & Warehouse	14
Internet Marketing	16
Wholesale Marketing	18
Private-Label Operations	20
Celebrity Endorsements	22
Corporate Citizenship	24
Finance & Cash Flow	26
Conclusion	28
About The Author	29

INTRODUCTION

As you probably already know, the Business Strategy Game, or BSG for short, is a business simulation game played by Business Administration, Accounting, and Finance majors to pass their capstone course from all over the world. Professors also use it for Master of Business Administration students like I had to do for my MBA. The simulation can be overwhelming and very time consuming without proper guidance and support. Because it is usually worth more than half of your grade, I wanted to write this guide to be that support, so you may feel comfortable making the game decisions to pass your final class.

This guide will go over essential topics that are important to making wise and strategic decisions. Keep in mind, **this is not merely a "put these numbers here, and you are guaranteed to win" manual.** Anyone who says you can follow certain decisions year after year and promise to win are most likely lying. Although there are specific strategies, you can implement throughout the game that should help you succeed in winning. I have played the game multiple times, once in the international Best-Strategy Competition. During these games, I have scored over 100 points for my G-T-D score. If you score above 100, I assume that most professors will give extra credit, as mine did for my MBA. I have also helped many other students by personally consulting with them. You are doing yourself a favor by reading this guide to save yourself time, stress, and headache. The topics below are things I wish I would have known before playing my first game. I hope you luck and let's dominate your competition.

SCORING

Most importantly, you need to know how scoring in the game works. BSG is a competitive game. You are competing against others in your class to win and survive the competition. Technically, all of you can probably pass, but you are fighting your classmates to pass at the end of the day. There will be winners and losers. You must take this game seriously if you want to pass the course and, better yet, become a champion and possibly get invited to the Best-Strategy Invitational.

There are five main criteria that you must focus on for scoring. They consist of earnings per share (EPS), return on equity (ROE), stock price, credit rating, and image rating. Each of these has two weighted scores that will, in turn, affect your overall game to date score, which is where your grade will come from typically. These two weighted factors are called investor expectation score and best in industry score. You may also get bonus points from the Bull's Eye award and Leap Frog award. Game to date score plus bonus points equals overall game to date score.

	Y11 (2.50)	Y12 (3.00)	Y13 (3.50)	Y14 (4.00)	Y15 (4.50)	Y16 (5.25)	Y17 (6.00)	Y18 (7.00)	Y19 (8.50)	Y20 (10.00)	Wgt. Avg. (5.43)	Y20 Score I.E. B-I-I	G-T-D Score I.E. B-I-I	
A	2.82	4.88	2.52	4.01	4.94	3.90	5.87	6.74	8.85	9.78	5.15	20 8	19 8	A
B	2.97	4.48	3.44	5.10	5.34	6.34	8.27	8.44	10.68	18.45	7.02	24 15	23 11	B
C	2.00	0.69	2.24	3.66	3.68	4.02	6.84	6.20	7.77	13.38	4.72	23 11	17 8	C
D	3.93	7.13	10.82	13.51	13.30	10.98	11.90	13.66	17.57	24.26	12.31	24 20	24 20	D
E	3.27	4.79	5.48	5.17	8.01	7.47	7.22	7.30	12.83	23.34	8.10	24 19	24 13	E
F	1.47	0.03	-2.68	-0.60	2.72	2.49	3.56	3.38	6.64	8.76	2.32	18 7	9 4	F
G	3.36	1.50	2.51	3.00	0.59	0.90	2.09	1.58	4.11	0.69	2.05	1 1	8 3	G
H	2.25	5.57	6.02	9.79	6.83	4.84	6.26	8.44	9.58	14.19	7.16	24 12	23 12	H
I	1.43	0.54	1.02	2.00	3.31	2.73	3.85	5.93	8.10	9.25	3.74	19 8	14 6	I
J	1.40	-0.99	1.76	2.38	1.80	0.92	0.80	0.17	2.82	-0.07	1.10	0 0	4 2	J

Investor expectation, IE, score is solely up to your company and doesn't get affected by your competitors. To score well in investor expectations, you must score higher than their annual benchmark, located in the parenthesis underneath Y11 and on. You can score up to 24 points for this section by being well above and beyond their expectation (approximately 40%). Best in industry, BII, score is based on how well your competition does. This metric changes based on the company with the highest score for a single year. For example, if company D scores $24.26 for Y20, other companies will have their score based on a percentage of that top score being worth the max points (20).

Now that you know how IE and BII work, I can go over the most crucial goal, having the best game to date score. G-T-D uses both EI and BII in its scoring method. It takes 50% from investor expectation and 50% from best in industry. You need to make sure that your game to date score is high to have the best chance at winning and receiving an excellent grade. I will now explain how to get high G-T-D scores in each criterion.

To get a good score in EPS, you must think long term. Each year is essential to keep above investor expectations and be the best in the industry because your G-T-D will be based on the weighted average, wgt. avg., of the past ten years. You will score well in IE by being above the weighted average, and you will have a good BII by being the best weighted average out of all companies. Like EPS, return on equity is another long-term scoring measure. You must make sure that you keep your ROE high year after year to produce the best G-T-D score.

The next is the stock price. This metric is vital on Y20 or Y15 if you are only playing for five years, as I have done before. The goal is to get this number on your final year to be as high as possible. After the stock price is the credit rating score. Here is probably one of the most straightforward categories to gain points. As long as you have an A+ in the final year, you should score all the points in this area. I have seen winning companies have low credit scores in years 12-15 to come up and make sure they have an A+ just in the final year. Lastly, image rating is different from all the rest. Image rating is scored based on a three-year rolling average ending with years 18,19 and 20. You must make sure these final years are high for a good score in image rating. I believe 100 is needed as your average score to gain the full 24 points in IE. A quick bonus tip, I have seen patterns in winning teams having good image rating throughout the ten years.

Image Rating

Image Rating scores are based on a 20% (20-point) weighting. A bolded number indicates achievement of the investor expected image rating shown below each yearly column head. A highlighted number indicates best-in-industry performance. Game-To-Date scores are based on an average of the most recent three years.

Y11 (70)	Y12 (72)	Y13 (72)	Y14 (75)	Y15 (75)	Y16 (77)	Y17 (77)	Y18 (80)	Y19 (80)	Y20 (80)	Y18-Y20 Average	Y20 Score I.E.	Y20 Score B·I·I	G-T-D Score I.E.	G-T-D Score B·I·I
83	74	79	83	81	86	87	79	79	84	81	21	17	20	16
81	73	59	69	67	73	78	79	89	59	76	15	12	19	15
71	67	69	67	62	66	67	60	61	67	63	17	13	16	13
85	98	100	100	100	100	97	100	100	100	100	24	20	24	20
83	80	83	89	99	93	100	90	93	92	92	22	18	22	18
74	74	66	73	77	78	84	80	78	78	79	20	16	20	16
68	74	69	70	83	81	77	69	55	58	61	15	12	15	12
94	100	100	100	92	84	90	87	83	75	82	19	15	20	16
71	75	83	79	84	83	91	98	99	95	97	22	19	22	19
55	47	66	63	64	61	52	54	56	55	55	14	11	14	11

The last two areas to gains some extra points are the Bull's Eye award and the Leap Frog award. The Bull's Eye award is given by being within specific percent variances in revenue, EPS, and image rating. Winning these awards are won by correctly changing your projections to be accurate to your year's actual results. It is harder said than done, unfortunately. The Leap Frog award is earned by the company with the most remarkable positive change in the year's score. I don't believe there is any correlation nor pattern for these bonuses leading to a team winning, but it can help.

The final thing I will discuss for scoring is corporate social responsibility spending and the CSR award. This award gives zero points to your final score. I would suggest aiming for above-average annual expenditure on this category to have a good bang for your buck in enhanced image rating, which does help win the game. That's it for how scoring works. If you want exact details, please read the help guides directly on the game. Next, I will discuss the best long-term strategy.

CHOOSING THE RIGHT STRATEGY

At the beginning of the class and game, you will probably have to discuss your company's strategy. Are you going to become a differentiated firm or low-cost provider? Should you enter Asia-Pacific or Europe-Africa? What quality of shoes and how many models should we have? These are all typical questions to ask, and I am going to help you solve them.

First and foremost, I suggest all companies be willing to change their strategy if the need arises. If you are going for low-cost and all the other companies go there too, you will probably want to switch to get a decent market share. When it comes to strategy, I believe it is most important to think of, "Where do we want to be on the competitive comparative efforts chart"? You have four options:

1) Low model / Low S/Q rating-price
2) Low model / High S/Q rating-price
3) High model / Low S/Q rating-price
4) High model / High S/Q rating-price

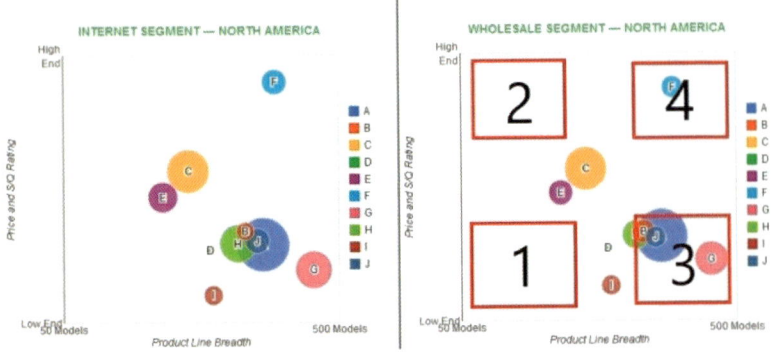

My suggestion is never to do option one. I haven't heard of anyone winning with that strategy. I would say that options 3 or 4 are the best to focus on, but you may be successful with option 2. From my experience, most winning companies are around the right side of the chart.

Now that you know what area of the chart you want to focus on, how will you get there? This is where you can decide if you will build production space in Latin America to have lower tariffs or differentiate your shoes with a higher S/Q rating. Maybe both? There are many different strategies your company can use to be successful, which makes BSG very interesting. I will not tell you exactly what approach is best because nearly any strategy has a chance to win at the end of the day. I will show you how to make the right decisions that coincide with options 3 and 4 to have the best chance at winning, in my opinion. We will now look at each decision screen to go over wise decision making.

*The below advice might not work well with option 2.

COMPENSATION & TRAINING

This section is probably one of the most laid back and straightforward areas to make decisions. First, you will want to keep the base wage between 0-2%. I don't see the benefit of raising it any higher per year. Incentive pay can be kind of tricky. You will want to put some money here but make sure your incentive pay as % of regular compensation is less than 25%. I usually keep fringe benefits at zero unless you want to make sure your employees are above average in total compensation, which could help productivity. Best practices are the bread and butter of this screen. This metric has long-term benefits, and I suggest you invest a decent amount into it. I do not recommend funding the max amount. You will want to play with the numbers and find where the investment increase lets you bump up in materials cost impact. For example, watch for Sup to go from -0.10 to -0.19. Choose one of those, and do not go in between. I suggest thinking about where you will be focusing your factories and investing more in areas you want to use in the long-term, like Asia Pacific. You can watch the total cost of production labor for supervisory staff as changing it to find which is the best. You can give a small percent increase in salary if you would like. Please don't think of this game as real-world employees and how they should psychologically work. Some people might want to give their employees massive raises because a real-world company did that. You will not like the results.

*As you make decisions, I suggest using your arrow keys on the keyboard. It will save you massive amounts of time.

Workforce Compensation & Training		North America Facility		Europe-Africa Facility		Asia-Pacific Facility		Latin America Facility	
Prior-Year Compensation and Productivity Data		Industry Average	Company G	Industry Average	Company G	Industry Average	Company G	Industry Average	Company G
Workforce Compensation (total $ per year)	Base Wages	35,658	36,067	21,228	0	12,727	12,986	12,446	12,487
	Incentive Pay	3,569	0	3,468	0	2,360	0	2,403	0
	Fringe Benefits	775	0	500	0	575	0	333	0
	Total Regular Compensation	40,002	36,067	25,196	0	15,662	12,986	15,182	12,487
	Overtime Pay (includes incentives)	8,097	10,823	7,121	0	3,504	3,897	2,748	3,742
	Total Compensation	48,099	46,890	32,317	0	19,166	16,883	17,930	16,229
Incentive Pay as a % of Regular Compensation		8.9%	0.0%	13.8%	0.0%	15.1%	0.0%	15.8%	0.0%
Workforce Productivity (pairs per worker per year)		5,463	4,756	3,893	0	3,815	3,414	3,842	3,538
Compensation and Training of Production Workers	Base Wage (% change from prior year)	Minimum Wage = 35,380		Minimum Wage = 21,228		Minimum Wage = 12,487		Minimum Wage = 12,487	
		0% ▼	36,067	+1% ▼	0	+1% ▼	13,116	+1% ▼	12,612
	Incentive Pay ($ per non-rejected pair)	$ 0.00 ▼	0	$ 0.00 ▼	0	$ 0.00 ▼	0	$ 0.00 ▼	0
	Fringe Benefits ($ per year)	$ 0 ▼	0	$ 0 ▼	0	$ 0 ▼	0	$ 0 ▼	0
	Total Regular Compensation ($ per year)		36,067		0		13,116		12,612
	Overtime Pay (includes incentives)		10,834		0		3,934		3,778
	Total Compensation ($ per year)		45,901		0		17,050		16,390
	Incentive Pay as % of Regular Comp.		0.0%		0.0%		0.0%		0.0%
	Best Practices Training ($ per worker)	$ 600 ▼	per worker	$ 0 ▼	per worker	$ 2400 ▼	per worker	$ 2000 ▼	per worker
	Materials Cost Impact (from cumulative expenditures)	Std -0.30	Sup -0.49	Std 0.00	Sup 0.00	Std -0.23	Sup -0.39	Std -0.06	Sup -0.09
Supervisory Staff (ratio of production workers to supervisors)		40 ▼ to 1	Staff = 5	50 ▼ to 1	Staff = 0	45 ▼ to 1	Staff = 39	50 ▼ to 1	Staff = 6
		Ind. Avg.	Co. G	Ind. Avg.	Co. G	Ind. Avg.	Co. G	Ind. Avg.	Co. G
Prior-Year Supervisory Compensation ($/year/supervisor)		63,865	63,036	37,091	0	26,172	26,265	25,758	25,758
		Minimum Salary = 62,436		Minimum Salary = 37,462		Minimum Salary = 26,016		Minimum Salary = 26,016	
Supervisory Compensation (% change in salary, benefits, and bonus)		0% ▲	63,036	0% ▲	0	0% ▲	26,265	0% ▲	26,016
Projected Workforce Productivity (pairs per worker in Y15)		4,734		0		3,423		3,640	
Number of Workers Employed (given branded production entries)		211		0		1,753		275	

		$000s	$/pair	$000s	$/pair	$000s	$/pair	$000s	$/pair
Cost of Labor Associated with Footwear Production	Production Workers — Base Wages	7,610	6.34	0	0.00	22,992	3.19	3,468	2.89
	Incentive Pay	0	0.00	0	0.00	0	0.00	0	0.00
	Fringe Benefits	0	0.00	0	0.00	0	0.00	0	0.00
	Overtime Pay	2,286	1.91	0	0.00	6,897	0.96	1,039	0.87
(Per-pair figures not adjusted for rejected pairs)	Total	9,896	8.25	0	0.00	29,889	4.15	4,507	3.76
	Best Practices Training Expenditures	127	0.11	0	0.00	4,207	0.58	550	0.46
	Supervisory Compensation (salary + benefits)	315	0.26	0	0.00	1,024	0.14	156	0.13
	Total Cost of Production Labor	10,338	8.61	0	0.00	35,120	4.88	5,213	4.34

BRANDED PRODUCTION

Here is where the game starts to get complicated. You will find yourself having to go back and forth to screens to make the right decisions. I will try my best to explain what you will most likely have to do on this decision screen without getting too complicated. To start, you will probably want to look at superior materials and enhanced styling and features. I suggest dropping both to zero at the start of each year if you're going to find the best combination. You will then go back and forth between them to find the best cost per S/Q rating mixture. Please pay attention to total branded production costs as you raise one of them like superior materials. Raise it to 2%. Did the S/Q rating go up 0.1 stars? If it did, what is the production cost after doing that? Now lower it back down to where it was at and raise enhanced styling. What is its production cost for that extra 0.1-star rating? By doing this, you will find the best mixture for the lowest price. Do this until you find a star rating you think will work best for your strategy.

Next, I will go over another long-term investment decision, TQM/Sigma Six. I usually like to spend a decent amount in this area as well. Like best practices training, you should probably put a little more into where your long-term factories will be. I don't suggest maxing the investment in TQM. I recommend staying below $4 unless you know you have the money to spend while keeping high EPS and ROE. Technically, best practices and Sigma Six have diminishing returns. Still, I assume you won't notice them until toward the end of the game if you invest an above-average amount.

The number of models/styles is a crucial factor in where you will be taking your company on the competitive chart. This number dramatically influences your total branded production demand for the year. If you do not have enough production to supply the market, you may want to use this to help decrease the need. You may also use advertising and pricing to lower demand or raise demand. I like to max out at 500 styles to gain the extra demand because you can increase the price to reduce that demand if you do not have enough factory space to produce the full amount needed.

Lastly, on this screen is deciding how many shoes in each factory you want to produce. You will most likely have to go back and change this multiple times as you progress through the decision pages. I would first go to private label and make sure you get what shoes you need there, and then you can go back to this page and use the rest for branded demand. Remember that you might want to prioritize the branded market because it might make more per shoe, however. Another critical factor is not to make a few shoes in one location. You will notice that your branded production cost will skyrocket if you are making a few shoes. That is why I will suggest focusing on production in only two or three facilities. One more quick thing you can change is the anticipated material prices. I usually don't touch this because it is challenging to predict what your competition will do, and it could mess up your projected numbers.

PRODUCTION FACILITIES

The production facilities page is another simple screen. Here you will decide what type of equipment to purchase, which I will suggest new equipment. You can also choose to sell old equipment. Selling equipment is wise if you plan on not using it that year and sometime soon. Money in hand is better than just sitting around and depreciating. The next area is deciding which improvement options to choose. You may only pick one per year, and the max is two per facility. Many people waste money here for not understanding how the screen works. For example, Option B is usually a no brainer to invest in because the capital outlay will be paid within a few years if you are doing the high model shoe strategy. You can see this by looking at the top number and dividing it by the bottom to get the payback period. The numbers will change over the years, but option B is usually a worthwhile investment and sometimes option A or C. The last decision is whether you want to add space or not. I suggest focusing on AP and LA. You will also notice that as you increase space, it gets cheaper per 1,000 of added space. I saw a pattern that most international winning companies had most of their space in AP and LA. You will want to add space when you feel that demand will be higher the next year, and you are close

THE BUSINESS STRATEGY GAME GUIDE

to already maxing out your current space.

EQUIPMENT FOR FOOTWEAR PRODUCTION	North America Facility	Europe-Africa Facility	Asia-Pacific Facility	Latin America Facility
Space Available for Footwear Production Equipment in Y15	5,000 pairs	1,000 pairs	8,000 pairs	2,000 pairs
Production Equipment in Place at Beginning of Y15 (000s of pairs)	1,000 pairs	0 pairs	6,000 pairs	1,000 pairs
Purchase of Production Equipment — New (000s of pairs) / Refurbished (000s of pairs)	0 / 0 pairs	0 / 0 pairs	0 / 0 pairs	0 / 0 pairs
Sale of Existing Equipment (oldest equipment will be sold first)	0 pairs	0 pairs	0 pairs	0 pairs
Total Footwear Production Capability in Y15 (000s of pairs without OT)	1,000 pairs	0 pairs	6,000 pairs	1,000 pairs
Percentage of New / Refurbished Production Equipment	100% 0%	0% 0%	33% 67%	100% 0%

PRODUCTION IMPROVEMENT OPTIONS		North America Facility	Europe-Africa Facility	Asia-Pacific Facility	Latin America Facility
Option A	Purchase of special equipment to reduce reject rate by 50% — Capital outlay ($000s) / Projected annual cost savings at current reject rate ($000s)	$2,500 / $1,508 — No	$0 / $0 — No	$15,000 / $2,090 — Done	$2,500 / $726 — Done
Option B	Layout revisions to reduce production run setup costs by 50% — Capital outlay ($000s) / Projected annual cost savings at current model count ($000s)	$1,600 / $3,590 — Done	$0 / $0 — Done	$9,600 / $2,915 — Done	$1,600 / $3,715 — Done
Option C	Purchase of special equipment to increase S/Q rating by 1 star — Capital outlay ($000s) / Projected annual cost savings at current S/Q effort ($000s)	$4,800 / $7 — No	$0 / $0 — No	$28,800 / $456 — No	$4,800 / $613 — No
Option D	Robot-assisted production to increase worker productivity by 50% — Capital outlay ($000s) / Projected annual cost savings at current production ($000s)	$14,400 / $1,859 — No	$0 / $0 — No	$86,400 / $1,323 — No	$14,400 / $-735 — No

SPACE FOR PRODUCTION EQUIPMENT	North America Facility	Europe-Africa Facility	Asia-Pacific Facility	Latin America Facility
Space in 000s of Pairs (without OT) — Equipment Space at the End of Year 14	5,000 pairs	1,000 pairs	6,000 pairs	1,000 pairs
Construction of Additional Space (initiated in Y14)	0	0	2,000	1,000
Space Available for Equipment in Year 15	5,000 pairs	1,000 pairs	8,000 pairs	2,000 pairs
Construction of New / Additional Space (to be available in Year 16)	0 pairs	0 pairs	0 pairs	0 pairs
Space Available for Production Equipment in Year 16	5,000 pairs	1,000 pairs	8,000 pairs	2,000 pairs

Capital Outlays in Year 15 ($000s)					
Purchase of New Equipment	$	0	$ 0	$ 0	$ 0
Purchase of Refurbished Equipment		0	0	0	0
– Book Value of Equipment Sold		0	0	0	0
Equipment Upgrade Options		0	0	0	0
Energy Efficiency Initiatives		375	0	2,250	375
New / Additional Facility Space		0	0	0	0
Net Capital Outlays in Year 15	$	375	$ 0	$ 2,250	$ 375

DISTRIBUTION & WAREHOUSE

Here is another decision screen that you will probably go back and forth multiple times. The goal here is to ensure all projected inventory surplus toward the bottom of the screen is at least +100 in each geographical area. Never have a shortfall here. You will be giving your competition-free sales. The first decision to make is whether to clearance any of last year's shoes. I usually suggest doing this if you can make a margin over cost. I will typically watch my net profit and EPS to see if they will change this number. You will also want to make sure you are changing this number while having a surplus in that area to make the projections work right.

Next, you will start to choose where you want to ship shoes. You always want to satisfy local demand with a local facility first. For example, if NA has -2,300, you will want 2,400 shoes from NA to stay there. The rest can go where you see fit based on exchange rate changes. A red number means that the game will decide where the shoes will go, and I don't suggest having this. Let's say you have a bunch of surplus shoes. I would put it into one or maybe two areas that you want to prioritize. You will then increase branded advertising as needed to find the best decision by watching if your net profit increases or decreases. I will explain more in Wholesale Marketing.

BRANDED DISTRIBUTION		North America Facility	Europe-Africa Facility	Asia-Pacific Facility	Latin America Facility
Pairs Available for Shipment (000s of pairs produced at each facility after rejects)		1,062 pairs	0 pairs	5,440 pairs	562 pairs
Pairs to be Shipped from Facility to (000s of pairs)	North America Warehouse	3400	0	0	0
	Europe-Africa Warehouse	1448	0	1036	0
	Asia-Pacific Warehouse	0	0	2775	0
	Latin America Warehouse	0	0	1600	515
Remaining Pairs to be Shipped (if left unshipped, will be shipped automatically)		3,766 pairs	0 pairs	29 pairs	47 pairs

WAREHOUSE OPERATIONS	North America Warehouse			Europe-Africa Warehouse			Asia-Pacific Warehouse			Latin America Warehouse		
	Pairs	Models	S/Q	Pairs	Models	S/Q	Pairs	Models	S/Q	Pairs	Models	S/Q
Inventory Left Over at the End of Year 14 (000s)	406	500	2.8★	303	498	2.6★	315	498	2.4★	243	495	2.0★
Inventory Clearance (prior to Year 15 operations)	0 ▾	%	0 pairs	0 ▾	%	0 pairs	0 ▾	%	0 pairs	0 ▾	%	0 pairs
	$000s	$/pair		$000s	$/pair		$000s	$/pair		$000s	$/pair	
Clearance — Discounted Clearance Revenues	0	0.00		0	0.00		0	0.00		0	0.00	
Statistics Direct Cost of Pairs Cleared	0	0.00		0	0.00		0	0.00		0	0.00	
Margin Over Direct Cost	0	0.00		0	0.00		0	0.00		0	0.00	
	Pairs	Models	S/Q	Pairs	Models	S/Q	Pairs	Models	S/Q	Pairs	Models	S/Q
Beginning Inventory (000s of pairs carried over from Year 14)	406	500	2.8★	303	498	2.6★	315	498	2.4★	243	495	2.0★
Incoming Shipments from — North America Facility (see Note 1 below)	3,400	500	3.1	1,448	500	3.1	0	0	0.0	0	0	0.0
Europe-Africa Facility	0	0	0.0	0	0	0.0	0	0	0.0	0	0	0.0
Asia-Pacific Facility	0	0	0.0	1,036	500	2.8	2,775	500	2.8	1,600	500	2.8
Latin America Facility	0	0	0.0	0	0	0.0	0	0	0.0	515	500	0.8
Pairs Available for Sale in Year 15 (see Note 2 below)	3,806	500	3.0★	2,787	500	2.8★	3,890	500	2.8★	2,358	500	2.3★
Projected Demand (given branded marketing decision entries)	3,951			3,214			3,322			2,502		
Required Inventory (needed to achieve delivery time)	140	(2-week delivery)		195	(2-week delivery)		363	(2-week delivery)		282	(2-week delivery)	
Projected Inventory Surplus (Shortfall)	-285	(minimal)		-622	(minimal)		-595	(minimal)		-426	(minimal)	

Projected Distribution and Warehouse Costs		$000s	$/pair	$000s	$/pair	$000s	$/pair	$000s	$/pair
Exchange Rate Cost Adjustment (on incoming shipments)		759	0.65	-727	-0.44	0	0.00	-2,866	-1.19
Distribution and — Freight on Footwear Shipments		759	0.65	2,730	1.64	2,790	0.90	3,780	1.57
Warehouse Tariffs on Pairs Imported		0	0.00	8,190	4.91	0	0.00	16,090	6.67
Costs Inventory Storage (on Y14 inventory)		204	0.18	152	0.09	158	0.05	122	0.05
Packaging / Shipping (Net + wholesale)		11,393	9.78	11,842	7.10	15,221	4.90	11,918	4.94
Warehouse Lease / Maintenance		1,000	0.86	1,000	0.60	1,000	0.32	1,000	0.41
Total Dist. and Whse. Costs		13,356	11.46	23,914	14.34	19,169	6.17	32,910	13.63

Note 1: These figures include the Pairs to be Shipped figures entered at the top of the page and their associated model availability and S/Q rating attributes. If all of the available pairs at a facility are not shipped then the unshipped pairs will be automatically shipped to regional warehouses in proportion to the shipping decision entries that exist for that facility.

Note 2: The number of models and S/Q rating of pairs available in each warehouse is a weighted average of the models and S/Q ratings of pairs in beginning inventory and of pairs shipped in from each plant. The weighted average model availability and weighted average S/Q rating in each region is used to determine the attractiveness of your brand against the brands of rival companies in the industry.

INTERNET MARKETING

This page can be simple, but you will most likely want to go back to this page after switching some things in Wholesale Marketing. To start, you will bring search engine advertising down to zero. I haven't seen the benefit of this being up, other than possibly when you have celebrities. Next, you need to think about how much demand you currently have. If you have a high supply of shoes, try adding free shipping. Does it raise or lower your EPS and net profit? If you don't have enough supply, you can raise prices to reduce demand, which will most likely also help your EPS. You're in a good position if you have much demand because you can easily tweak numbers to lower demand while raising profit. Don't sell in a location where your operating profit is negative. Try to increase the price if that is the case, or don't supply there. Lastly, I wouldn't mess with the competitive assumptions unless you are confident about how they will change. Finicking with assumptions could mess up your projections and eventually cause your actual metrics to be way off.

*Always make sure your retail price exceeds wholesale price by 40%.

THE BUSINESS STRATEGY GAME GUIDE

INTERNET MARKETING

		North America Market		Europe-Africa Market		Asia-Pacific Market		Latin America Market	
		Year 14	Year 15	Year 14	Year 15	Year 14	Year 15	Year 14	Year 15
Marketing variables generated by production and marketing decisions in Y15	S/Q Rating (weighted average)	3.1★	3.0★	2.9★	2.8★	2.7★	2.8★	2.3★	2.3★
	Models Available (weighted average)	500	500	498	500	498	500	495	500
	Brand Advertising ($000s)	20,000	20,000	16,500	16,500	15,000	15,000	10,500	10,500
Internet Marketing Decisions	**Retail Price** ($ per pair sold online)	82.00	82.00	90.00	90.00	76.00	76.00	89.00	89.00
	Retail Price Exceeds Wholesale Price by	40%	40%	40%	40%	41%	41%	40%	40%
	Search Engine Advertising ($000s)	7,000	7000	6,000	6000	0	0	0	0
	Free Shipping (from warehouse to buyer)	No	No	No	No	No	No	No	No
Marketing variables determined by prior-year decisions / outcomes	Celebrity Appeal (sum of appeal indices for all celebrities under contract)	60	245	45	260	100	270	65	200
	Brand Reputation (prior-year image rating)	72	72	72	72	72	72	72	72
		Year 14 Actual	Year 15 Projected	Year 14 Actual	Year 15 Projected	Year 14 Actual	Year 15 Projected	Year 14 Actual	Year 15 Projected
Internet Market Share (% of total regional sales volume)		12.0%	13.7%	11.0%	12.9%	10.9%	12.9%	9.3%	10.3%
Internet Sales Volume (000s of pairs sold to online customers)		675	858	531	700	463	631	371	476
		$000s	$/pair	$000s	$/pair	$000s	$/pair	$000s	$/pair
Revenue, Cost, and Profit Projections for Year 15	Gross Internet Revenues	70,356	82.00	63,000	90.00	47,956	76.00	42,364	89.00
	± Exchange Rate Adjustments	0	0.00	3,364	4.81	2,225	3.53	5,906	12.41
	Adjusted Gross Revenues	70,356	82.00	66,364	94.81	50,181	79.53	48,270	101.41
	+ Shipping Fees (paid by customer)	10,725	12.50	8,750	12.50	7,888	12.50	5,950	12.50
	Net Internet Revenues	81,081	94.50	75,114	107.31	58,069	92.03	54,220	113.91
	Cost of Pairs Sold	26,434	30.81	21,093	30.13	13,012	20.62	14,443	30.34
	Warehouse Expenses	11,733	13.67	9,297	13.28	8,154	12.92	6,201	13.03
	Marketing Expenses	27,664	32.24	17,472	24.96	6,957	11.03	5,565	11.69
	Administrative Expenses	2,139	2.49	1,745	2.49	1,573	2.49	1,187	2.49
	Operating Profit (Loss)	13,111	15.28	25,507	36.44	28,373	44.97	26,824	56.35
	Operating Profit Margin	**16.2%**		34.0%		48.9%		49.5%	
Estimated industry averages are entered on the Wholesale Marketing decision entry page.	S/Q Rating	5.2★		5.2★		5.2★		5.3★	
	Models Available	347		351		339		336	
	Brand Advertising ($000s)	$ 12,450		$ 9,050		$ 10,100		$ 6,550	
Competitive Assumptions	Retail Price ($ per pair)	$ 81.65 ▲		$ 84.70 ▲		$ 77.70 ▲		$ 86.60 ▲	
	Search Engine Advertising ($000s)	$ 5375 ▲		$ 4750 ▲		$ 4200 ▲		$ 2725 ▲	
	Free Shipping	▲		▲		▲		▲	
Industry averages for these non-price marketing decisions are determined by prior-year decisions / outcomes	Celebrity Appeal	111		109		110		111	
	Brand Reputation	73		73		73		73	

Competitive Assumptions: Enter your estimates of the industry average marketing efforts that will prevail in each internet segment in Year 15. The more accurate your estimates are, the more accurate your projected market shares and unit sales will be.

WHOLESALE MARKETING

This page is the most complex. It connects many of the other pages and will require you to go back and forth many times, most likely. First, I suggest you bring brand advertising to zero in all locations. Then, you need to make sure you have distributed your shoes appropriately on the distribution page, or else making changes here will be pointless. Once you even out your shoes to locations, you can start to see what you will want to change by looking at the surplus or shortfall. For example, if you have a shortfall of -500 in NA, you should go to internet marketing to raise the NA price. Raise it $1 and then go back to this page and raise it here $1 or whatever is best to make it, so you do not turn retail outlets red. You can raise it more at a time if you wish. Do this until the shortfall turns into a decent surplus if you have, for example, +1,000 in NA. Then you can go to brand advertising and start raising in using the arrow keys on your keyboard. Watch the net profit percent in your projections to see when it becomes highest. Unfortunately, there are many possible combinations to make that will affect projected shoes in an area. I hope by now you know enough about the game to go to the necessary pages and make the appropriate decisions. After you work on pricing and brand advertising, you can start switching mail-in rebates and delivery time to see what produces the best EPS, ROE, and net profit increase. You want to make sure that you have above-average retailer support. Having retailer support helps you with next year's demand levels. Do not put this down to zero until the final year, possibly to get a boost to EPS and ROE. Also, I would suggest not selling in a geographical location where your operating profit is negative. Lastly, as I said in other pages, I do not recommend messing with competitive assumptions unless you are sure to where they will change.

PRIVATE-LABEL OPERATIONS

Private label operation is a decision page that you may come back to a few times, depending on how much you are playing with the rest of the numbers. Here your focus is to get shoes in all areas cheaply to provide a reasonable bid price that isn't the lowest and not the highest. I suggest finding how many shoes you need in each place first. For example, you will send 500 shoes from NA to NA and see the projected private-label market share. If it is red, you probably should decrease the number until it turns gray. You will do the same for the AP facility. Ship 500 to EA, AP, and LA, then find the sweet spot for how many you need in each. Once you do this, you can add up the totals you need to send in each facility and then go back to Branded Production. Subtract the total you got from private label from total production capability. The number is how many shoes you can make in each facility for branded demand.

Once you have how many shoes you need, you can finish the page. Change enhanced styling to $0 and use superior materials to raise your star rating in each facility to the global minimum. Then you will want to look at the comparative competitive efforts report in each location to see what price your opponents are most likely going to

THE BUSINESS STRATEGY GAME GUIDE

sell their private label. You need to make sure you get the bid, so try to be a decent amount below them, but not the lowest. Also, do not lose money by selling for a loss. If your margins are negative, you probably shouldn't sell there unless they are small and you have a bunch of profit. Selling for negative margins would be solely to get extra image rating. Lastly, make sure you set the red boxes on the bottom to "yes" if you are positive, you will win them.

PROPOSED PRIVATE-LABEL PRODUCTION			North America Facility	Europe-Africa Facility	Asia-Pacific Facility	Latin America Facility
Private-Label Specifications	Materials	Standard Materials %	78 %	50 %	68 %	0 %
		Superior materials %	22	50	32	100
	Number of Models / Styles (global requirement)		100 models	100 models	100 models	100 models
	Enhanced Styling / Features ($000s per model)		$ 0 /model	$ 28 /model	$ 0 /model	$ 6 /model
S/Q Rating of Private-Label Pairs to be Produced (Global Minimum = 4.2★)			4.1★	0.0★	4.2★	4.2★
Capacity Available for Private-Label Production (000s of pairs)			0 pairs	0 pairs	1,425 pairs	590 pairs
Private-Label Pairs to be Produced and Shipped to (before rejects)		North America Warehouse	0	0	0	0
		Europe-Africa Warehouse	0	0	625	0
		Asia-Pacific Warehouse	0	0	675	0
		Latin America Warehouse	0	0	125	590
Proposed Total Production of Private-Label Pairs (000s of pairs)		Regular Time	0 pairs	0 pairs	225 pairs	390 pairs
		Overtime	0	0	1,200	200
		Pairs Rejected	0 (4.0%)	0 (0.0%)	48 (3.4%)	31 (3.3%)
		Net Private-Label Production	0 pairs	0 pairs	1,377 pairs	559 pairs
Projected Cost of Private-Label Pairs to be Produced ($ per pair)			$0.00 per pair	$0.00 per pair	$20.95 per pair	$22.39 per pair

PRIVATE-LABEL CONTRACT OFFERS		North America Market	Europe-Africa Market	Asia-Pacific Market	Latin America Market
Private-Label Demand (projected total regional demand assuming non-fully competitive conditions - see page 4 of FIR)		3,360 pairs	3,360 pairs	3,670 pairs	3,670 pairs
Pairs Offered for Sale (to be produced and shipped if offer is accepted)		0 pairs	604 pairs	652 pairs	680 pairs
Price Offer (must be at least $10.00 below the Y15 regional average wholesale price)		$ 38.50	$ 43.99	$ 37.25	$ 43.35
Projected Private-Label Market Share (if offer is accepted)		0.0%	18.0%	17.8%	18.5%
		$000s $/pair	$000s $/pair	$000s $/pair	$000s $/pair
Revenue, Cost, and Margin Projections for Year 15	Gross Private-Label Revenues	0 0.00	26,570 43.99	24,287 37.25	29,478 43.35
	± Exchange Rate Adjustments	0 0.00	1,419 2.35	1,127 1.73	4,109 6.04
	Net Private-Label Revenues	0 0.00	27,989 46.34	25,414 38.98	33,587 49.39
	Production Cost	0 0.00	12,654 20.95	13,659 20.95	15,051 22.13
	± Exchange Rate Adjustments	0 0.00	-101 -0.17	0 0.00	-230 -0.34
	Freight / Packaging / Tariffs	0 0.00	5,436 9.00	1,304 2.00	2,691 3.96
	Margin Over Direct Costs	0 0.00	10,000 16.56	10,451 16.03	16,075 23.64
The projected outcome of winning a Private-Label contract may be included in the overall performance projections for the current year. Select "Yes" for a region only if there is a reasonable probability of winning a Private-Label contract in the region.		Incorporate the projected outcomes for this region into Y15 projections? No	Incorporate the projected outcomes for this region into Y15 projections? Yes	Incorporate the projected outcomes for this region into Y15 projections? Yes	Incorporate the projected outcomes for this region into Y15 projections? Yes

CELEBRITY ENDORSEMENTS

Celebrities are useful for increasing your company's demand. I highly suggest trying to get at least two or three celebrities. Do not overspend in the beginning years. I have seen people pay $15,000 or more within the first few years, and it is way too much. I think between $1,000 and $3,000 should be enough to get some celebrities in the beginning years, but it depends on your competitors' willingness to pay for celebrities. It would be best if you didn't have to terminate a contract early unless you paid a crazy amount for a celebrity. You should base prioritization on which geographical area you want to focus on, like LA or AP. You can make a simple Excel spreadsheet and find celebrities with the best average total points. Put a spending cap if you want to make sure you only pay a certain amount for that year to obtain celebrities.

CELEBRITY ENDORSEMENT CONTRACTS

Celebrity	Appeal Indexes				Currently Signed By	Contract Amount ($000s / yr)	Terminate Contract Early	Contract Length	Available for Offer	Contract Offer ($000s / yr)	Offer Priority
	N.A.	E-A	A-P	L.A.							
Judy Judge	85	65	60	40	C Company	2,800		2 years	NOW	$ 0	
Kimmie Jimmel	100	70	65	75	Achilles Footwear	5,000		2 years	NOW	$ 0	
Bud Birkenstock	70	100	70	55	C Company	2,800		2 years	NOW	$ 0	
Jose Montana	60	50	60	95	DShoelebrity	1,500		2 years	Year 16		
Samuelle Jackson	40	85	60	100	Achilles Footwear	7,000		3 years	Year 17		
Bronko Mars	60	45	100	65	Icon Shoes	600		3 years	Year 17		
Steff Caraway	75	80	95	60	G exclusive shoe Com	4,502	No ▼	3 years	Year 17		
Jay XYZ	75	70	55	90	Achilles Footwear	7,000		3 years	Year 17		
Nunchuck Norris	90	80	100	65	G exclusive shoe Com	4,502	No ▼	2 years	Year 16		
Roger Federation	75	85	65	100	E Galaxy Footwear	3,000		3 years	NOW	$ 0	
Nick Shavan	70	75	70	55	F Yeah!	2,500		2 years	NOW	$ 0	
Anderson Blooper	65	60	70	80	F Yeah!	3,300		3 years	Year 16		
Mic Jagermeister	80	100	75	75	G exclusive shoe Com	4,502	No ▼	2 years	Year 16		
Jim Hardball	65	45	70	70	F Yeah!	2,000		3 years	Year 16		
LaBron Game	100	80	85	85	Achilles Footwear	7,000		2 years	Year 16		

Spending Cap on Year 15 Contracts ($000s) $ 0   When the total annual cost of the company's winning Year 15 contract offers reaches this dollar amount, all remaining lower-priority offers will be withdrawn. $0   Sum of Year 15 contract offers

Most Recent Contract Offers
(letter in parentheses indicates company that made the offer)

Celebrity	No. of Offers	Highest Offer	2nd Highest	3rd Highest
Judy Judge	3	2,800 (C)	2,000 (G)	500 (I)
Kimmie Jimmel	4	5,000 (A)	2,800 (C)	2,500 (G)
Bud Birkenstock	3	2,800 (C)	2,500 (G)	500 (I)
Jose Montana	4	4,502 (G)	2,000 (F)	1,500 (D)
Samuelle Jackson	6	7,000 (A)	4,502 (G)	3,000 (C)
Bronko Mars	4	4,502 (G)	2,000 (F)	600 (I)
Steff Caraway	4	7,000 (A)	4,502 (G)	3,000 (C)
Jay XYZ	4	7,000 (A)	4,502 (G)	2,500 (C)
Nunchuck Norris	5	4,502 (G)	4,000 (D)	3,700 (C)
Roger Federation	3	3,000 (E)	3,000 (A)	1,000 (F)
Nick Shavan	4	2,800 (C)	2,500 (F)	2,000 (G)
Anderson Blooper	3	3,300 (F)	2,000 (G)	2,000 (C)
Mic Jagermeister	3	7,000 (A)	4,502 (G)	3,200 (F)
Jim Hardball	3	2,800 (C)	2,000 (G)	2,000 (F)
LaBron Game	6	7,000 (A)	4,502 (G)	4,000 (D)

- Enter all contract offers in thousands of dollars per year. For example, enter an offer of $2.5 million as 2500.
- The minimum annual contract offer is $500k (entered as 500).
- A contract offer entry of $0 for a given celebrity indicates that the celebrity will receive no offer.
- The maximum annual contract offer is $30 million (entered as 30000).
- In a given year, offers may be made to as many celebrities as are available, however a company will be awarded no more than 3 celebrity contracts in the same year.
- When making offers to multiple celebrities in the same year, it is recommended that you prioritize the offers and set a spending cap for the year (to guard against winning more contracts than intended).
- In a given region, the maximum affective celebrity appeal total is 300. When the sum of the appeal indexes in a given region reaches 300, no additional market impact is gained by signing more celebrities.

CORPORATE CITIZENSHIP

On this page, you will want to focus on having above-average spending than your competition. I don't suggest trying to be the highest spender unless you have the cash and profit to do it. Focus on energy efficiency initiatives and charitable contributions. I believe these have the most significant effect based on what the player guide suggests. Save both improved working conditions for your final year to get a bump in EPS and ROE, most likely. You may spend money on other initiatives if you would like, but make sure you aren't overspending because this page only helps with image rating. You do not get any bonuses for winning the CSR award.

THE BUSINESS STRATEGY GAME GUIDE

Corporate Social Responsibility and Citizenship

Below are seven CSRC initiatives that can be used to develop a "social responsibility strategy" for your company. The drop-down selection boxes below offer several optional actions.

While undertaking CSRC initiatives is often considered "the right thing to do," one reason to operate in a socially responsible manner is to enhance the company's image. Aggressive and astute pursuit of a social responsibility strategy over 5 years can increase the company's Image Rating by 15 to 20 points.

Which (if any) of the seven initiatives to pursue and how much to spend is entirely voluntary. There is no pressure to spend anything on these initiatives — the company can perform successfully without undertaking any social responsibility initiatives in Year 10; prior company management spent no money on any of the seven optional social responsibility initiatives.

The Help button at the top-right offers further information and guidance regarding the seven CSRC initiatives.

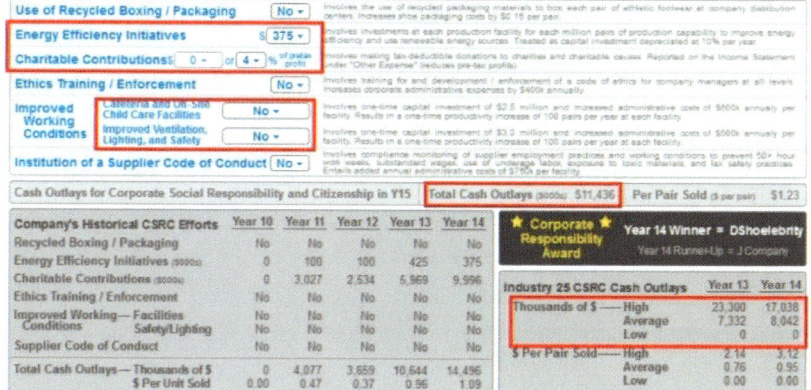

FINANCE & CASH FLOW

At last, the final decision page. Here you will want almost always to buy back the max amount of stock possible. Unless it is very highly-priced, nearly all top international winning companies had 15,000 shares in year 20. I believe it is a must to have the best chance at winning. You will not be able to buy back shares if you are less than $15 per share. I suggest never issuing stock because it will make it very difficult to reach 15,000 shares by the end of the game. Don't pay dividends until towards the end of the game when you have extra cash on hand. Taking out loans is entirely ordinary and usually necessary. I would stick to five- and 10-year loans. Also, don't be afraid to pay off old high-interest rate loans with lower interest rate loans. Keep your projected cash balance high enough so that the bar is not colored yellow or red. Usually, it is around $20,000 or higher.

THE BUSINESS STRATEGY GAME GUIDE

FINANCE AND CASH FLOW

Sources of Additional Cash ($000s)
- 1-Year Bank Loan (5.80% interest): $0
- 5-Year Bank Loan (6.30% interest): $0
- 10-Year Bank Loan (6.80% interest): $0
- Stock Issue (000s of shares at $241.31): 0
  - Maximum share issue in Y15 = 5000k

Uses for Excess Cash ($000s)
- Early Repayment of L-T Loans (Balance Sheet Note): None — N/A
- Dividend (/share): Year 14 dividend was $0.00 — $0.00
- Stock Repurchase (000s of shares at $241.31): 0
  - Maximum share repurchase in Y15 = 1493k

Shares of stock outstanding at the *beginning* of Year 15: 18,095 k
Shares of stock outstanding at the *end* of Year 15: 18,095 k

Projected Cash Available in Year 15 — $000s

Beginning Cash Balance (carried over from Year 14)		$37,976
Cash Inflows — Receipts from Footwear Sales		715,597
Bank Loans — 1-Year Loan		0
5-Year Loan		0
10-Year Loan		0
Stock Issue (0 shares @ $241.31)		0
Sale of Used Production Equipment		0
Interest Income on Y14 Cash Balance		1,063
Loan to Cover Overdraft (1-year loan @ 7.8%)		0
Cash Refund (awarded by instructor)		0
Total Cash Available from All Sources		**$754,636**

Projected Cash Outlays in Year 15 — $000s

Cash Outlays — Payments to Materials Suppliers		$78,549
Production Expenses (excluding depreciation)		102,497
Distribution and Warehouse Expenses		98,780
Marketing and Administrative Expenses		145,762
Capital Outlays — Facility Expansion (new space)		0
Equipment Purchases		0
Equipment Upgrade Options		0
Energy Efficiency Initiatives		3,000
Bank Loan Repayment — 1-Year Loan		0
5-Year Loans		23,000
10-Year Loans		0
Interest Payments — Bank Loans		7,130
Y14 Overdraft Loan		0
Stock Repurchases (0 shares @ $241.31)		0
Income Tax Payments		58,040
Dividend Payments to Shareholders		0
Charitable Contributions		8,061
Cash Fine (assessed by instructor)		0
Total Cash Outlays		**$524,819**

This positive cash balance could generate interest income of $6.4M in Year 15.

Projected Cash Balance at the End of Year 15 ($000s): $+229,817

Other Important Financial Statistics

	Last Year	Year 15 (projected)
Interest Rate Paid on Overdraft Loans	8.3%	7.8%
Interest Rate Received on Cash Balances	2.8%	2.8%
Shareholder Equity (mandated minimum = $150 mil.)	$431 mil.	$566 mil.

Performance on Credit Rating Measures

	Last Year	Year 15 (projected)
Interest Coverage Ratio (operating profit ÷ interest exp.)	48.67	34.22
Debt to Assets Ratio (total debt ÷ total assets)	0.25	0.16
Risk of Default (based on Y15 default risk ratio of 0.90)	Low	Low

CONCLUSION

I hope that this guide has been informative and helpful for you to win your Business Strategy Game. I have tried my best to explain how to work through each page logically and effectively to get a great score. As a reminder, the game has many different strategies and ways to win. It would be near impossible for me to walk you through how to win each of them. You should still read the player guide and use the help guides provided. This guide is not a step by step way to win the game, although it will be helpful to refer to until you get the hang of making decisions. Good luck with dominating your competition!

ABOUT THE AUTHOR

Derek J. Barnick

Derek Barnick excels in business and finance. He scored in the 99th percentile on the Major Field Test for a Master's in Business Administration (MBA) out of approximately 17,000 students, scored in the 92nd percentile on the Major Field Test for a B.S. in Business Administration out of approximately 68,000 students, and tied for 5th out of 43 international teams in the 2020 Best-Strategy Invitational. Derek is a certified Financial Modeling and Valuation Analyst. He also creates helpful YouTube videos for students and entreprenuers.

Feel welcome to reach out to him at djbarnick@gmail.com or on social media.

Printed in Great Britain
by Amazon